T0208956

No Works!...
No Faith!

Vicki L. Baker CMBC, CELC, CPC

BALBOA.PRESS

A DIVISION OF HAY HOUSE

Balboa Press books may be ordered through booksellers or by contacting:

Balboa Press
A Division of Hay House
1663 Liberty Drive
Bloomington, IN 47403
www.balboapress.com
1 (877) 407-4847

Scripture taken from the King James Version of the Bible.

Scripture quotations taken from The Holy Bible, New International Version® NIV® Copyright © 1973 1978 1984 2011 by Biblica, Inc. TM. Used by permission. All rights reserved worldwide.

Scripture taken from the Amplified Bible, Copyright © 1954, 1958, 1962, 1964, 1965, 1987 by The Lockman Foundation. Used with permission.

Scripture taken from The Message. Copyright © 1993, 1994, 1995, 1996, 2000, 2001, 2002. Used by permission of NavPress Publishing Group.

Scripture taken from The Expanded Bible. Copyright ©2011 by Thomas Nelson. Used by permission. All rights reserved.

Print information available on the last page.

ISBN: 978-1-9822-3911-4 (sc)
ISBN: 978-1-9822-3912-1 (e)

Balboa Press rev. date: 11/23/2019

Dedication

I dedicate this book to my amazing and supportive husband Avery, who I truly love and have been married to for 39 years. Your encouragement has helped me more than you'll ever know. To my beautiful loving daughters Tramaine and Shawntel, I'm so proud of you and all of your accomplishments. I love you both. Last but not least, much love to my Dad (Jesse), Mom (Elaine, who has transitioned) and my Sister (Varina), my Son in love (Ben) and brother in love (Warner). I appreciate the prayers, love and support!

MY STORY

J ust like some of you, I was raised to get an education so I would be able to get a good job, and that's exactly what I did. I eventually landed a job that I really liked in the hospitality industry, and quickly became a supervisor/global trainer. I enjoyed what I was doing. I thought that I would be there forever.

One morning I came into work and was called into a meeting. There in the meeting, were all of the VP's and upper management. I thought to myself, something's about to happen, since the VP's all lived out of state and there wasn't any notification of them coming to visit. Well, it wasn't long after the meeting began, that we were told that our center was being closed down and that we could prepare to leave immediately. My heart dropped. So, I went back to my desk and started clearing it out. My team started looking at me and asking me what was going on? I told them you'll find out in a minute. As people started finding out that their jobs were being eliminated, you could hear crying around the whole center. I will never forget that day.

As you can imagine, I was devastated and was wondering what my next move would be. Although, I had the opportunity to relocate, but due to my mom's illness and other reasons, I chose not to. I felt numb and thinking to myself, here I am, (at the time) age 57, what am I going to do now? I thought to myself, "Wow, 12 1/2 years at this place, now what?

So, after the initial shock of my job closing, I decided to pursue my Coaching business. I was already Certified as a Life Coach, and I also became Certified as a Master Business and Executive Leadership Coach. As an Ordained Minister, I worked with youth and women, and have held many conferences, so coaching was natural for me. I absolutely love it!

I always had faith that I would have a successful and prosperous coaching business. Although I was able to be a blessing to many, my business still wasn't growing as I thought it could. So, I took a leap of Faith. I took my severance pay and invested in myself and studied under some of the most amazing legendary thought leaders in the Personal Development industry. I felt that if I were to be the best, then I wanted to study under the best, and that is exactly what I did. I attended their conferences and was so moved that I even became a consultant for one of them

I truly enjoyed working with individuals and businesses, and they've expressed how I made a difference in their personal and professional lives, but for some reason it seemed like I couldn't help myself. I began applying what I had learned from the programs/conferences, and I started seeing manifestations here and there in my own life, but not on a consistent basis. As I watched my bank account decreased, I had to ask myself what was I doing wrong? I understood the universal laws, or at least I thought I did. I also had to asked myself, how is it even possible to have helped so many others and not be able to help myself? I eventually got to a point where I knew that I would have to re-enter the workforce. I needed a steady income. I just couldn't figure out what I was missing or doing wrong. I was praying and believing, and I just knew that I was operating in Faith.

During this time, I was at one of the lowest points in my life. I felt like the bottom had dropped out from under me. I was doing everything that I thought I should be doing, speaking what I wanted to see in my life, visualizing how I wanted my life and coaching business to look, but I still came to this point. So, I made a decision to re-enter the workforce in the field that I absolutely was good at.

On September 1st, I started submitting resumes and I open myself to possibilities outside of my area. I was totally focused. I knew that if I were to share my decision with others, right away it would be a lot of questions that I would have to answer. This would have attracted negative energy to me, so I kept my decision to myself. I had a strong feeling and I knew in my inner being that within 15 days I would have confirmation of working back in hospitality industry. I didn't know how, I didn't know where, but I had a strong feeling that it would happen, and for the first time in my life I trusted myself and my inner being completely. I was totally focused. A lot of things transpired in those 15 days, but I stayed the course. I followed the divine direction within me, and on September 15th, I receive confirmation that I would be working again in the hospitality industry, (exactly 15 days from when I applied). I was excited about this manifestation!

What I realize on this journey I'm on, is that in the past, I had too many things going on. Even though I had attracted things into my life, it wasn't on a consistent basis because my energy was spread all over the place. I had several goals and I kept changing my mind. Scripture says in *James 1:8 (KJV), that a "Double minded man is unstable in all his ways."* That was me, double minded. I've learned that I needed to focus all of my energy on one thing at a time, at least that's what worked for me. I had no other goal, nothing else on my list, but to be back working in the hospitality industry in 15 days and that's exactly what happened. The job that I manifested was in another state, so I ended up relocating, it was a very quick move. While I thought I was moving for the workplace, I suddenly realized that God had another plan. I now understand that, I was able to create this job for myself, by not only having faith, but by working it and becoming a deliberate creator. I've learned when you want to see something come into your life, you can't wish for it or just hope for it, you have to expect it.

Although the job was going fine, and I was back in the hospitality industry, I felt a deep calling inside of me to do more than I was doing, so I began coaching again. This time from a whole new perspective!

As I was working with my clients, I began to seek God for divine direction. During this time of seeking, I really started paying attention to my faith-based community. I couldn't help but notice that so many people seemed to look outside of themselves for their desires to be met. Let me explain, some believe that when they pray, that God will do it for them, and they wait and wait, but what they fail to realize is that God is in them and working through them to accomplish all that they have prayed for. In other words, it's already done! Others believe that someone or something outside of them will make things happen for them, they have even allowed outside circumstances to dictate how they live their lives. But I have learned differently.

It was through this revelation that I became aware of what the deep calling inside of me was and wanting to be expressed. It was helping people understand that just having faith wasn't enough, there is action involved. According to *James 2:17 (AMP) "So too faith, if it does not have works [to back it up], is by itself dead [inoperative and ineffective]."* The Two (Faith) and (Works) are One.

I believe the reason so many people are not seeing the manifestations of their faith, is because they do not completely understand how to work their faith. Scripture says in *Proverbs 4:7 (KJV) "Wisdom is the principal thing; therefore, get wisdom: and with all thy getting get understanding."*

With the wisdom I received, I have a better understanding of how to work my faith, and keep it alive and I want to share it with you.

In this book is my experience and what was revealed to me by God. I understand that everyone may not be in agreement with my interpretation of scripture as it relates to Faith, Works and Universal Laws. But it's my hope that through my words, you too, will be able to discover for yourself, how to keep your faith alive, so you can be, do and have whatever you desire.

In all of your getting,
get an understanding

Chapter One

KNOW YOURSELF...

A lthough I believe that there is Truth everywhere, I like to begin with one of my favorite scriptures…. "In all thy getting, get an understanding."

My belief is that Life is in the interpretation of the words in scripture. And if we learn how to interpret scripture so that it will bring us life, then we will not live a defeated life.

I truly believe that everyone has the answers within themselves, it's just a matter of discovering them. The discovery of these answers may shock you at first, then you'll be amazed by what you have discovered. You may find that the "Truth" that has been revealed to you, may be completely different from what you have been taught and what you have become to know as "Truth."

Let me warn you! When you begin your journey of real, self-discovery, it may be a lonely journey. You may find yourself thinking so differently from how you use to think. You'll want to share your thoughts with others, but they won't have a clue of what you're talking about. Don't be shocked when what you thought you knew begins to change. You will start seeing things from a totally different viewpoint. On this journey you have to know your truth. Not the truth that we may have been raised to believe. Not your Mother and Father's truth, but yours. You have to ask yourself the question, "What do I really believe?"

We have to be willing to unlearn so we can relearn. In other words, we have to reprogram ourselves. Since I've began questioning everything, I've noticed some things that I used to believe in, wasn't exactly working in my favor. As a Certified Master Business, Executive Leadership and Life Coach, I've studied a lot in the personal development space. I've always wanted to be the best for my clients, so I began applying what I learned into my life. I begin to see things differently. Never before have I understood the Law of Attraction so clearly.

Growing up in a traditional church, I never heard "Law of Attraction" being discussed. As you can imagine, as a minister, when I saw the laws of attraction throughout scripture, I changed my mindset and allowed myself to explore beyond what I was taught. I challenged myself to let go of beliefs that were no longer serving me. I allowed myself to be free from the opinions of others. I allowed myself to let go of what was and focused on a new, or better yet, a different way of thinking.

We are going to have to allow ourselves to move from what was. Begin today with a new way of thinking. Renew your mind (*Romans 12:2 AMP*). It's okay to start over again and again, until you feel comfortable with the decisions that you make for your life. Some of us have been living the life that others have determined for us, even from childhood. Now it's time to discover what's good for you. You've helped everyone succeed and be the best they could be, now it's time to be selfish and focus on yourself. It could mean reprogramming yourself and starting all over again, and you know what "It's Okay"! It will take some time to unlearn many years of things that were taught to you. Have patience, the relearning will be well worth it.

I've discovered that the kingdom of God is within me and outside of me. In other words, we must know who we are as creators of our own reality, then we will see the manifestations of our desires. As scripture says, " ...A tree is ·known [identified; recognized] by the kind of fruit it produces." (*Matthew 12:33 EXP*). How we think of ourselves from within, shows up in our experience on the outside.

We're connected to the most powerful source within. The universe is always ready to respond to our commands. Life is for us and never against us. When we are connected within, we can send and receive all kinds of information using thought and imagination. I call this my innernet.

Now the **Internet** is the worldwide web and it's how we operate in the universe outside of us. The **InnerNet** is how we operate inside of us.

When we are connected to the "Internet" outside of us, we are governed by the laws of the outside world. We tend to see and speak about things the way the world does.

When we are connected to the "InnerNet" inside of us, we are governed by the laws and principles from within. We see the world from the inside, through our thoughts and Imagination.

Imagination is powerful. Everything you see around you was created from someone's imagination. If they can do it, so can we.

When I discovered how powerful I am and that the laws of the universe were in scripture, it caused me to change my mind and my way of thinking. That's why It's so important while you are on your quest, your journey, that you keep seeking until you find what you're searching for. It doesn't matter if its wealth, health or a better life, whatever you desire comes from within.

I've found out that it was more important for me to be at peace with how I thought and the decisions and choices I make for my life. I came to a point, and you may too, that the only opinion that matters is your own. Your own TRUTH! What is true for you may not be true for anybody else, and that's ok.

I believe there are many paths to a destination and you must find yours. The road is truly narrow, but it's your journey through life and not anyone else's. Just be and do you.

Chapter Two

UNDERSTANDING THE "WORKS"

Faith without Works is Dead...

James 2:17 Amplified Bible (AMP)
17 So too, faith, if it does not have works [to back it up], is by itself dead [inoperative and ineffective]

I n order to fully operate in Faith, and see the manifestations of what we are believing for, then according to this scripture, "Faith" by itself isn't enough. Therefore, "Faith" and "Works" must be unified and work in harmony with one another. I like to think of it as a union where the "Two becomes One" or better yet, the "Two" are indeed "One." There is a union, a marriage, a partnership so to speak, between "Faith" (belief) and "Works" (action-universal laws) that cannot be ignored, and you must apply both to experience the manifestations of your desires.

There are laws that govern us in the physical realm. If we break these laws, we are subject to being handcuffed, arrested, restraint and even locked up. Our freedom could be taken away. There are also laws that govern our spiritual realm, and I call them "universal laws." Now with these laws, if you break them, you are subject to feeling bound, stuck, fearful and worried. Preventing all good from flowing to you. We must be law abiding citizens, before our "Works" can back up our "Faith."

So, let's talk briefly about universal laws, these laws govern our spiritual realm. First of all, we are vibrational (spirit) beings, living in a body. We have a body, but we are not our body. If we are to abide by these laws, so that we are not bound, stuck, fearful and worried, then we must first understand the laws and how to operate with them. The universal laws are the action or the (works) component in Faith.

Let me share another story how I applied the "works", universal laws, to tip the scale in my favor. I recently had some medical tests done, because I was feeling some kind of way in my body. When the test results came back, it showed me that some of my numbers were out of alignment and not in my favor. It was at this point when I made a conscious decision to take control of my health, by using positive thought and energy. I was not on medication and I told my Dr. that I didn't want to be on any. I told her that I would get my numbers back in alignment naturally. I knew that it was going to take the same energy that I used to manifest other things, to reverse these test results. I like to call this "tipping my scale."

When I speak of Tipping my scale, I'm speaking of applying the works to my Faith and controlling my situation. My health, My Wealth, My Life, My Career, etc. I began to understand that everything in our life starts out evenly. 50% is the situation that's presented itself and 50% is our belief about that situation. I thought about the law of polarity, which states that, "Everything in the universe has its opposite." For example, you have a right and left side, a front and back etc. The law of Polarity not only states that everything has an opposite ...it is equal and opposite. If something you considered bad happens in your life, there has to be something good about it. Remember that we make a situation what it is by the way we look at it. When you look at the situation one way and it is negative, you can change your viewpoint and see it as positive. This is what I had to do. Even though the test results weren't favorable, I looked at it from a different perspective. I knew that this was the wakeup call I needed to begin eating better. Before the test results, I had struggled all year long, trying to find the right diet to go on to lose or release weight. I tried everything, All meat one day, counting points the next, Vegan on another day and Vegetarian the next. You name it, I had tried it. So, after receiving my test results, I immediately had a mindset change and decided that I was going to change and look at this situation from a positive perspective. I tipped my scale.

In order for us to change any situation, or any concern we must learn how to Tip the scale in our favor. Some of you have given up on dreams, because your scale tipped in the wrong direction. You were going to start a business, but you let circumstances take control and your scale started tipping in the wrong direction. You have career aspirations, but you've talked yourself out of going for the position. You've allowed negative influences to tip you in the wrong direction. You've started on your purpose journey, but some blocks showed up and you've allowed discouragement to tip you in the wrong direction and stop you from pursuing your dreams. You may have even, shared your thoughts with others and you allowed their negative opinions to tip you in the wrong direction.

I found out that, all it takes is just 51% to tip your scale in the direction of health from sickness, from lack to abundance, from sadness to joy and whatever else you are struggling with. That extra 1% makes all the difference in your life. People may say you're crazy for believing the way you do, but the only thing I've found that is crazy was my limited belief and not having a full understanding on how to apply the works to my Faith. That extra 1% in the right direction can change everything. So, I focused all of my energy on tipping the scale in the direction of better health. I visualized every test result being in alignment. I also change the way I was eating and within a week, I saw a change.

In this Faith walk, you are going to have to understand how to apply the "Works" of the universal laws to see the manifestations of what you are believing for and tip every scale in the direction you want to see.

Let's review again, *James 2:17- Amplified Bible (AMP) - 17- "So too, faith, if it does not have works [to back it up], is by itself dead [inoperative and ineffective]."* These laws must coincide with each other. By operating with the laws (works), this is what brings the manifestation of your desires into your experience. Your understanding of how "Faith" and "Works" work together is what keeps your "Faith" alive.

Chapter Three

FAITH UNDER PRESSURE

James 1:3-4 The Message (MSG)
"2-4 Consider it a sheer gift, friends, when tests and challenges come at you from all sides. You know that under pressure, your faith-life is forced into the open and shows its true colors. So, don't try to get out of anything prematurely. Let it do its work so you become mature and well-developed, not deficient in any way".

Without pressure or contrast there can be no clear choices. The reason for this is because the pressure of what we don't want, causes us to ask for what we do want. Once we ask for what we want the universe (works) is on it, making things happen. The asking causes the universe to answer, this is what we call deliberate creation. Being a deliberate creator will cause you to make decisions about what you want in your life. Depending on the decision we make, will determine the pressure we may experience, in order to keep our faith alive.

We have to make a decision on what we want for our lives, nothing will happen until we make a decision. Once a decision is made then the direction for us to go in, will be shown. The direction may be shown through our impulses, that gut feeling. When you experience this feeling, it could be your intuition guiding you. It's very important to act upon your intuition at the time you receive it. Don't put it off, don't wait. By waiting, you may miss your opportunity to create your desired life or the thing that you are expecting. The universe has already put in place all the components we will need along the way. Trust the process and know that our desires will show up and become a reality at the appropriate time.

Right here, I'm reminded of a decision I decided to make. This was truly Faith under pressure. As I stated in an earlier chapter, On September 1st, I started submitting resumes to re-enter the hospitality industry. What I didn't mention was the pressure on me to Keep my Faith alive, during the process. I came across some obstacles before I received confirmation of my job. One of the obstacles was the background check. Since I was able to monitor the status of my background check, one day I notice one area hadn't been verified. This was a concern because I was already hired, but could not begin work until the background check was completed. I felt a strong urge to contact the company to see what was the hold up. I waited and then I began to feel the urge again. I decided to call the company that was doing the background check. I was surprised to find out that the holdup was due to the hurricane that had happened in Puerto Rico. I was given a phone number to call and advise to call the company that I was being employed with to tell them about the hold up. So, I called and spoke to someone at the company. The gentleman that I spoke with had no idea that the hurricane in Puerto Rico was the hold up. He completely understood and contacted the background check company for verification, and within a couple of hours, I received an email confirming that the background check cleared and I was able to begin employment. Had I waited or procrastinated, the person I needed to speak with may not have been available. It was all about the timing. When your faith is under pressure, it's important to stay focused and in tuned with your inner being. Follow the divine direction from within.

Now, knowing that the pressure of problems brings solutions and asking brings answers, just trust that the universe knows where everything is to fulfil your desires. Make sure you don't continue to look for problems instead of solutions. Trust the process.

Working your Faith

Chapter Four

THE "WORKS" OF VISION

L aw of Attraction - simply put, law of attraction states that your thoughts determine your experience. In other words, your thoughts turn into things. You attract what you think about, whether you want it or not.

Habakkuk 2:2-The Message (MSG)
2-3" And then GOD answered: "Write this. Write what you see. Write it out in big block letters so that it can be read on the run. This vision-message is a witness pointing to what's coming. It aches for the coming—it can hardly wait! And it doesn't lie. If it

seems slow in coming, wait. It's on its way. It will come right on time."

You and I are spiritual beings we are creators of our own reality. Imagination is your God given vision for your life. Nothing outside of you creates. All creation comes from within. That said everything that we see in physical form, has already been created by someone like us. The vision for your life comes from within. We often lose focus of that insight when we allow outside circumstances to dictate how our life should be.

In Other words, everything that was created was because someone went inside themselves and created it there first. They had a vision, an idea, they imagined it. They thought about it and the thoughts created a feeling. Feelings are emotions and those emotions releases an energy out into the universe and the universe begin to immediately start to work on that person's behalf.

Right here I would like to break down this passage of scripture, into 3 parts, which I, in my opinion, believe to be the foundation for the Law of Attraction.

First Part, - Habakkuk 2:2-The Message (MSG)
2-3 And then God *answered: "Write this. Write what you see. Write it out in big block letters so that it can be read on the run."*

I believe that this is the beginning of the universal "Law of Attraction." It begins with your imagination. What do you see, what is God showing you? What dreams do you have? What are you emotionally connecting to? Here's how to apply the "works" of vision. Write down what you see and what's being shown. Write it in big block letters, so you can see and read it, during those times of doubt and discouragement. This could also be in the form of a vision board. Find pictures or quotes that will support what you see internally. Write down every detail. Step by step. What are you doing in your vision? Who's with you? What do you see? What do you hear, etc? Don't leave anything out.

Second Part - "This vision-message is a witness pointing to what's coming."

Remember that you must see it in your mind before it becomes a reality for you. What you see is the vision message as a witness, pointing to what's coming. This is so powerful when you really think about what the word "witness" means. Let's use marriage as our example, when you get married, they ask if you have a witness. Someone to confirm the two individuals have come together to begin their future together as one.

Again, according to *James 2:17 (AMP) "So too faith, if it does not have works [to back it up], is by itself dead [inoperative and ineffective]."* Then the "vision-message" is also a witness to faith and works joining together and becoming one to create whatever you are desiring. A confirmation to what is going to show up in your life.

When we think about the role of a witness, in regards to the physical laws, a witness must make an oath or solemnly state that they tell the truth in court. That said, with this universal law, the vision message is also making an oath or solemnly stating that what we see within ourselves, our imagination is the truth.

Third Part - "It aches for the coming—it can hardly wait! And it doesn't lie, if it seems slow in coming, wait. It's on its way. It will come right on time."

Delay is not denial. Most of the time, when our desires seem slow in coming, it could be to allow us time to get into alignment with our desires.

When I speak of alignment, this is where the universal law of vibration kicks in. You see, thoughts become things and you attract things to you based on the vibrations you release in the universe. The law of vibration is the foundation of the law of attraction. After the thought, you must become emotionally connected to the thought. This emotion is feelings and feelings are vibrations. Just that simple.

In other words, the way you feel is a vibration. The sound you release through your words is a vibration, the clapping of hands, etc. Vibration is an energy. It's with this vibration that God spoke the world into existence, *Hebrews 11:3 The Message (MSG)- 3 "By faith, we see the world called into existence by God's word, what we see created by what we don't see."*

You and I must be in the same frequency as the thing we are desiring. You can look at frequency as being on the same radio station as the music we want to hear. If I want to hear jazz, then I won't be able to hear jazz if I'm on a country station. Right? I must be in the same station or frequency as Jazz music, if I want to hear Jazz music. That's why we may experience a delay in receiving our desire. We must be in alignment and on the same vibration/frequency of what we're believing for. Scripture states, *"It aches for the coming—it can hardly wait! And it doesn't lie, if it seems slow in coming, wait. It's on its way. It will come right on time."* Our desires want to show up in our experience, but it can't show up, until we are in alignment and ready for it.

Writing your Vision Statement (Works)

It's important to have a "Personal Vision" and "Business Vision" statement. When writing your Personal statement, make sure that you are in a quiet place where you can focus and will not be interrupted.

Whatever decision you made to move forward in your life, make sure that you see yourself doing exactly what you want to do. Living how you want to live and having whatever you want to have.

Make sure that you're writing in present tense. According to *Hebrews 11:1- Amplified Bible (AMP) – "Now faith is the assurance (the confirmation, the title deed) of the things [we] hope for, being the proof of things [we] do not see and the conviction of their reality [faith perceiving as real fact what is not revealed to the senses]."*

This is what I did. First, I found a quiet area

- I sat back and closed my eyes
- I envisioned myself writing this book

- I saw myself conducting conferences/workshops to help people understand the partnership of "Faith" and "Works"
- I saw myself doing group and individual life coaching
- I could go on and on!

Now what do you see?????

- Visualize every detail
- It's your movie of the life you desire
- See yourself in the starring role
- What are you doing?
- Where are you going?
- How are you living?
- Who are you with?
- What does it feel like?
- What does your life look like? Etc.

Read what you wrote daily and throughout your day

Remember *Habakkuk 2:2-The Message (MSG)*
2-3 And then GOD answered: "Write this. Write what you see. Write it out in big block letters so that it can be read on the run. This vision-message is a witness pointing to what's coming. It aches for the coming—it

can hardly wait! And it doesn't lie. If it seems slow in coming, wait. It's on its way. It will come right on time."

This is how you apply the "works" of vision to keep your Faith alive.

Chapter Five

THE "WORKS" OF ASKING

Matthew 7:7 New International Version (NIV)
⁷ "Ask and it will be given to you; seek and you will find; knock and the door will be opened to you."

I also like the version that states, "the one who asks will always receive and the one who searches will always find."

When you ask, don't waver in your thoughts. Trust and know that it has already been done. We are asking from the belief and understanding that you're already in possession of it.

Notice the scripture didn't say "hope and it is given." or "wish and it is given. It says to ask and it will be given. On the flip side of that scripture it didn't say it would be on hold.

It didn't say, ask and it will be on layaway, which means you and I already have what we've asked for.

You must be very clear and confident in your asking. Don't worry about how it's going to happen, that's not your concern. Know that whatever you ask for will show up in your experience. It has to, according to, *Isaiah 55:11 Amplified Bible (AMP)-11 "So will My word be which goes out of My mouth; It will not return to Me void (useless, without result), Without accomplishing what I desire, And without succeeding in the matter for which I sent it."*

After you know what you want, you will have to do the research to find out how to get what you desire. This is what I call "Seek and you shall find." Once you make a decision then the way will be shown. To get to your vision, there are steps you have to take along the way. When you are seeking, you are actually doing research to see what you need to do to reach your goal.

You may want to look at the achievements of other people who are in the space you desire to go, find out how they got there, and what steps did they take. This by no means, is an indication that you will have to do the same thing, but by seeking and doing your research, you'll discover the steps you have to take or the goals you have to set in order to accomplish your desires. The action plan below will help get your started planning your "Staircase to Success."

"Staircase to Success" action plan.

- Make a list of everything it's going to take to get what you desire
- From that list, get another piece of paper
- Put your goal on the top line
- Starting from the bottom enter the first step you need to take
- On the line right above that, list the next step, so on and so on

This is your pathway to purpose.

You have a divine purpose guidance system within you that works like a GPS in a car. The GPS in a car asks you where are you now and where do you want to go? It never asks you where you were yesterday or even in the last hour. That's the same type of system you have on the inside of you. Your divine purpose guidance system just wants to get you from where you are now to where you want to be.

With each step you take, you are getting closer and closer to your goal. On this "Staircase" you'll know what to ask for and you will find that you'll begin to attract to you the people and resources needed to keep you focus on the big picture while you're on your journey.

Now there will be doors of opportunities all around you. It's one thing to knock on the door, it's another thing to open the door. Don't be concern if you "knock on a door". It just means it wasn't your door. You have to get through the "no's" in order to get to the "Yes." *Mark 11:24- Amplified Bible (AMP)-* ^{24} *For this reason I am telling you, whatever you ask for in prayer, believe (trust and be confident) that it is granted to you, and you will [get it].* This is how you apply the "works" of asking to your Faith.

Chapter Six

THE "WORKS" OF THINKING

Romans 12:2 Amplified Bible (AMP)
2 *"And do not be conformed to this world [any longer with its superficial values and customs], but be transformed and progressively changed [as you mature spiritually] by the renewing of your mind [focusing on godly values and ethical attitudes], so that you may prove [for yourselves] what the will of God is, that which is good and acceptable and perfect [in His plan and purpose for you]."*

Philippians 4:8-The Message (MSG)
8-9 *"Summing it all up, friends, I'd say you'll do best by filling your minds and meditating on things true, noble, reputable, authentic, compelling, gracious—the*

best, not the worst; the beautiful, not the ugly; things to praise, not things to curse. Put into practice what you learned from me, what you heard and saw and realized. Do that, and God, who makes everything work together, will work you into his most excellent harmonies"

The law of thinking state – "We attract what we think about." The way you think has everything to do with the working of your faith. What I mean by that is this, everything begins with a thought. *Proverbs 23:7- Amplified Bible (AMP) -* [7] *"For as he thinks in his heart, so is he…."*.

At this point, I would like talk about the **T.E.A.M.** There are a lot of breaks downs of this acronym, but I broke it down as (**T** - Thought, **E** - Emotion, **A** - Attracts, **M**-Manifestations). It's important to understand when working with "Faith", it's all about being in alignment with that which you are believing for. Your **"T**houghts" create a feeling and connects with an **"E**motion" inside of you. This emotion releases an energy, good or bad. This energy goes out into the universe and

"**A**ttracts" back to you what you are feeling, and this is what shows up in your experience or "**M**anifestation."

As Spirit beings, we are creating all of the time, whether we know it or not. We attract what we think about. We must understand that our inner being is pure positive energy and this energy feels good, when we are thinking positive thoughts. This energy connects with our emotions, our feelings, and they let us know when we're in alignment with our desires and that we're on the right path.

The "works" of thinking always let us know when we're out of alignment by the way we feel. When we feel negative or bad or any emotion opposite of our desires, then we're out of alignment. Which means that we have stopped or held up, the universe from releasing our desires back to us.

When I speak of alignment, I would compare it to driving a car. When you are driving and your car begins pulling right or left, it often indicates that your wheels are out of alignment and you need to have them checked. You'll find yourself, adjusting and turning the wheels, so you can remain in your lane. The same holds true when you are out of alignment with your inner man, who knows the desires of your heart. When you find yourself thinking thoughts that are negative or does not line up with your desire, then you must get back into alignment by changing your thoughts.

With this understanding of how thoughts create things, it's important that we become deliberate creators. You have to realize that, you can't think negative thoughts and expect to attract a positive response. You can't have abundance, when your focused thoughts are on the lack of money you have right now. You get what I'm saying?

By meditating and focusing on the "works" of your thoughts, just as *Philippians 2:13* stated, this will prevent you from allowing outside circumstances, environments and other people's opinions to create your reality. You do have control over your thoughts. This is how you apply the "works" of thinking to your Faith.

Chapter Seven

THE "WORKS" OF GRATITUDE

1 Thessalonians 5:16-18 Amplified Bible (AMP)
16 "Rejoice always and delight in your faith; 17 be unceasing and persistent in prayer; 18 in every situation [no matter what the circumstances] be thankful and continually give thanks to God; for this is the will of God for you in Christ Jesus."

When you begin on your journey and you want to manifest things into your life. You must have an attitude of Gratitude. Feelings of Gratitude puts you in a vibration of happiness, and joy. Gratitude gives you a peace that passes all understanding. It's from this state of being that

I am able to manifest my desires. I must be happy where I am, in order to get where I want to go. The "works" of gratitude keeps you in alignment with your desire. Even if you get off course, once you begin to think about your purpose, this thinking brings about an emotion of happiness and joy, and before you know it, you're back in alignment with your inner man.

When I'm grateful, it doesn't matter what my current situation is, because I know that all things are always working together for me. I'm not anxious or worried about anything. Being grateful allows me to have patience. *Philippians 4:6 Amplified Bible (AMP) states,* **6** *"Do not be anxious or worried about anything, but in everything [every circumstance and situation] by prayer and petition with thanksgiving, continue to make your [specific] requests known to God."* This is how you apply the "works" of gratitude to your Faith.

Chapter Eight

THE "WORKS" OF WORDS

Now that we have our goals established and we understand the importance of being in a state of gratitude. Let's speak to your vision. *Proverbs 18:21 The Message (MSG) - **21** "Words kill, words give life; they're either poison or fruit—you choose."*

Always remember that No word spoken is without power. That said, I would like to talk about, "Affirmations." The definition of "Affirmation" is the act of confirming something to be true, or is a written or oral statement that confirms something is true.

When it comes to your God given vision and the goals you've set. It's important to watch your words carefully. Always, speak positively to yourself and speak in the presence tense. Affirmations keeps you in alignment with your vision. The spoken word to yourself, reminds you of the "vision-message" that's a witness pointing to what is coming, as stated in *Habbakuk 2:2*.

When I write affirmations, I like to break down my affirmations, in the following way. "Who," "Does What," "By When." Who (being you), Does what (is what are you going to do), By When (is your goal date).

My affirmations look something like this.

Who... (is "I" or "My Brand" Also note: whatever you put after the word "I AM," you become)

I am a Certified Master Business, Executive Leadership and Professional Coach. I develop trainings/workshops and team building exercises for business and ministry needs. As a Spiritual life coach,

I help people create and develop a plan to achieve their dreams and goals.

I AM

- A co-creator with God, a minister and teacher of God's word
- A unique creator of trainings, workshops, conferences, teachings and coaching
- A magnet and all invitations for trainings, workshops, conferences, teachings and coaching are drawn to me.
- A money magnet and thousands of dollars are making its way to me
- A lender and not a borrower
- Persistent and focused and will not stop
- A best-selling author

Does what... (what I do)

- Hold conferences, workshops and trainings
- One on one coaching sessions
- Create team building workshops for ministries and businesses
- Teach, Coach and mentor

By when...(my goals)

- I am so happy and grateful now that between today and January 31, 20__, my books sales exceeded _____.

Use your "Staircase to Success" to create your affirmations. Every step you entered, make it a positive affirmation in the present tense. Affirmations keeps you going in the right direction. Make them personal and emotionally connect with what you're speaking over your life. You must feel it. Remember that you are releasing energy into the universe and it will return back to you, just how you released it. Keep in mind, *2 Corinthians 5:7 Message Version (MSG) - 7 It's what we trust in but don't yet see that keeps us going.* This is how you apply the "works" of words to your Faith.

Before we leave this chapter, let's take a look at another law, the universal law of cause and effect states that for every effect there is a definite cause, likewise for every cause, there is a definite effect. Your thoughts, words, and actions create specific effects that manifest and create your life as you know it. I'll close with this, *Isaiah 55:11 Amplified Bible (AMP)-11 "So will My word be which goes out of My mouth; It will not return to Me void (useless, without result), Without accomplishing what I desire, And without succeeding in the matter for which I sent it."*

Closing

I trust that you have been blessed by this powerful little book. James 2:17 Amplified Bible (AMP) states, **17** *"So too, faith, if it does not have works [to back it up], is by itself dead [inoperative and ineffective]."*

With this scripture we understand that having "Faith" by itself isn't enough. We must have the "works" to back up our "Faith." My desire and my hope is that you have a better understanding on how to apply the "Works" to your "Faith" so you can be, do or have whatever you are believing for.

Blessings,

Minister Vicki L. Baker CMBC, CELC, CPC

Contact information.
Email: Vicki@NoworksNofaith.com

About The Author

Vicki is a Minister and Certified Master Business, Executive Leadership and Life Coach. She is the CEO/Owner of Create Beyond Coaching, and also a Motivational Speaker. As a Life Coach she notice that many people were struggling in the area of their Faith. So she began to do a deep, study of "Faith without Works." Vicki discovered that the "Works" were actually the Universal Laws, found in Scripture. It was important for Vicki to share with you, the reader, what God has shown her. Vicki's desire is to show people how to apply these Laws to their Faith, so they can be, do and have whatever they are believing for.

Printed in the United States
By Bookmasters